Reincarnation

reincarnation

Edited with Introduction
and Commentary by
Brother Phap Luu

Thich Nhat Hanh

Parallax Press
**BERKELEY,
CALIFORNIA**

Illustrations
by Jeanne Fries

Published by
Parallax Press
PO Box 7355
Berkeley, California 94707

Parallax Press is the publishing division of
Plum Village Community of Engaged Buddhism
© 2025 Plum Village Community of Engaged Buddhism
All rights reserved

Cover and interior design by Katie Eberle
Illustrations by Jeanne Fries

Printed in Canada by Marquis

Parallax Press's authorized representative in the EEA is
SARL Boutique La Bambouseraie
Point UH, Le Pey, 24240 Thénac, France
Email: europe@parallax.org

ISBN 978-1-952692-97-0
Ebook ISBN 978-1-952692-98-7
Library of Congress Control Number: 2025942615

1 2 3 4 5 MARQUIS 29 28 27 26 25

The hermit Gautama smiled,
and whispered to himself, "O jailer, I see you now.
How many lifetimes have you confined me in the
prisons of birth and death? But now I see your face
clearly, and from now on you can build no more
prisons around me."

THÍCH NHẤT HẠNH,
Old Path White Clouds

Contents

Introduction

This book is an invitation into a new way of looking at your life and the events happening within
and around you. It presents the penetrating vision
of Zen Master Thích Nhất Hạnh—who we refer
to from here on by the Vietnamese name "Thầy,"
meaning monk or teacher—on the notions of birth,
death, and rebirth.

The thresholds of birth and death have
inspired ritual, religion, philosophical reflection,
and even political regimes. To look deeply into the
nature of birth and death requires courage and
perseverance. It is essential, at all points, that we
keep an open heart and an open mind. As Thầy
often reminds us, for the truth to penetrate and
reveal itself we must be willing to see our notions
for what they really are: constructs of our mind
that have a real effect on the present moment and

our future. We have to be willing to throw away all our concepts.

In the twentieth century we took a hard turn towards the doctrine of an individual self. We tend to think of who we are as an identity. But the reality is that any concept we or others have of ourselves is just a concept. Our body and mind are impermanent, and we find ourselves always in profound interdependence with all phenomena. In Zen, we are invited in every moment to observe the impermanence of the processes within our physical bodies—skin cells flaking off, wrinkling skin, graying hair, aches and pains that come and go. Our cells are being born and dying in every moment. Without death, how could life be possible?

We may have a harder time accepting the same phenomena of impermanence on a larger scale—at the level of our body itself. We have a natural drive to survive and a twin fear of the cold harshness of death. In his own time, the Buddha saw how this fear led to us being caught in the idea that our body, feelings, thoughts, emotions, and consciousness are our "self." He witnessed human beings caught like this being driven to inflict terrible pain, suffering, and violence on themselves and on each other through wars, murder, sexual assault, and other forms of violence. This drive to preserve the body at all cost continues to plague us today: we remain obsessed with life extension, health supplements, and technologies such as cryogenics that aim to preserve our physical body as long as possible, if not forever. We want to freeze our body, or a part of our body, like our head, in the hope that future civilizations will have the technology to revive us. Some of us see old age, sickness, and death as an illness we just don't yet know how to cure, like cancer, diabetes, or AIDS. We've become so cut off from the natural rhythms of life and death that we are no longer aware of what and who we are.

In this way, clinging to permanence drives our hopes and fears—about life and death, and rebirth. This clinging brings about a superficial understanding of rebirth; namely, that a permanent self, or soul, moves from one body to another— the so-called "transmigration of souls." We think that if rebirth is mentioned in Buddhist texts, this is what's being proposed: the passage of a soul from one body to another. And for some of us, this supernatural belief becomes an obstacle to taking Buddhist practice seriously.

In fact, Buddhist teachings on impermanence and non-self are much deeper and more subtle than this, as we will see in the pages that follow. According to Buddhist teachings, everything at every level of experience is of the nature to change. Everything is flow—and yet we are capable of guiding that flow. That is the path. That is how we ensure a beautiful continuation. Letting go of self and embracing impermanence helps us understand karma and continuation—our true rebirth.

The passages that follow have been selected by Matthew Friberg and I from Thầy's numerous talks and published works. In each chapter, to help the reader, I have added explanation of Thầy's ideas. The final chapter adds insights regarding how a right view of birth, death, and rebirth—i.e. the deeper view of continuation—can inspire us to practice Right Diligence and appropriate attention, bringing us happiness here and now, and on into the future.

These teachings, if applied, can bring us closer to the heart of reality and peace, and on a collective level can heal our fractured world. May this profound Dharma teaching benefit all beings.

BROTHER PHÁP LƯU

"What happens when we die?"
is a good question. A good answer should be
based on evidence. It's not a matter of belief
or faith, but of looking deeply. Through the
practice of mindfulness, concentration, and
insight, we can see for ourselves the true
nature of birth and death.

❊

Many people misunderstand the word
reincarnation, so I don't like to use it. The
word suggests that there is a soul, a spirit,
that exists apart from the body. And when the
body is destroyed or decomposed, the soul
leaves and searches for another body to enter.

I prefer the word continuation to the word
reincarnation. There is nothing that leaves
something and enters something else—
continuation is constantly taking place.

This is a very exciting subject to study.

THÍCH NHẤT HẠNH

1

Karma and Continuation

IMAGINE A TEAPOT. We put some tea leaves into the pot, pour boiling water in, and after waiting a few minutes, we pour out the tea. That tea is the continuation of the tea leaves. As the tea is drunk, we can see that the tea is in us, the teacup, and the person drinking the tea. When that person who drinks the tea writes poetry or calligraphy, we can also see the tea in the poetry and calligraphy. The tea is on a journey; it doesn't stay in one place.

When a person has a thought, it is their continuation. When that thought arises, it influences that person and their environment. The same is true of speech and bodily action: if we speak a word or perform an action, that word or action immediately affects us and our environment. In every moment, we generate energy in these three areas: thinking, speech, and bodily action. This is called karma, or action. Karma is our continuation, and continuation is rebirth. Every moment is a moment of rebirth.

We Are the Sum of Our Actions

We must see that we are not just within the boundaries of our five *skandhas*.[1] We are in all our karma, all our output. Output does not only mean going out but also moving forward. All our actions

---

1 According to Buddhism, a human being is composed of five skandhas: form, feelings, perceptions, mental formations, and consciousness. Form means our body, including our five sense organs and our nervous system. The second skandha is feelings; feelings can be pleasant, unpleasant, or neutral. The third skandha is perception, which includes noticing, naming, and conceptualizing. The fourth skandha is mental formations. According to the Vijñānavāda school of the northern transmission, there are fifty-one categories of mental formations. This fourth skandha consists of forty-nine of these mental formations; feelings and perceptions are mental formations, but because they are so important, they have their own categories. The fifth skandha is consciousness.

of body, speech, and mind are heading towards the future. When the French philosopher Jean-Paul Sartre said that a person is the sum of their actions, he was absolutely correct. It means that a person is the totality of all their karma, of their actions of body, speech, and mind. The karma they create affects both themselves, their five skandhas, and their surroundings. We must see that a person is both within and beyond the boundaries of skandhas, just as we see that the tea is not only in the teapot: it is also in the teacup, the person drinking the tea, and the poems and calligraphy they create. These are all different manifestations, expressions, of the fruits of our action.

Taking Care of What Comes In

The teapot is a useful image, but it is not perfect. We only see the tea going out, not coming in. However, in each moment of daily life, there is both input and output. We need to acknowledge that what we receive is a form of nourishment. What we hear, see, smell, taste, and feel all enter us at every moment. For instance, if we read a newspaper article, the sadness, anger, irritation, or violence of the article goes into us. That is called input.

Input in terms of the teapot would be tea and boiling water, but in terms of a person it can include many things: the air we breathe, the water we drink, the food we eat, the smells, images, and sounds that enter through our senses. The quality of the output depends a lot on the quality of the input. As we receive, so shall we create. If we consume a lot of violence and hatred, then what we create through body, speech, and mind will also contain these elements. If what we take in is wholesome, then what we create will be healthy. If we receive thoughts, images, and sounds that are kind, beautiful, and true, then with those materials we can create good karma for the future.

We must practice mindful consumption, guarding the six senses so that what goes into us does not harm us and become the source of harmful outputs. If we protect ourselves, the karma we create will be right karma, good karma. Guarding the six senses means placing a guardian at each sense gate—eyes, ears, nose, tongue, body, and mind—to be aware of what is entering the citadel of the skandhas. That is mindfulness. The guardian at the six gates is our mindfulness.

Things that go in through our five skandhas are, in fact, just raw materials. If we have a practice, a path, we can transform whatever we receive into something beautiful. For example, if we lack wisdom and mindfulness when we watch a violent film, the energy of violence will enter us and harm us. What we produce, how we express ourselves, and how we behave will then contain those violent elements. But if we practice, our mindfulness and concentration will protect us. Those elements enter us, but we can transform them into understanding, compassion, and the path itself. It's like the silkworm that eats mulberry leaves: when it spins silk, it does not produce mulberry leaves; it produces silk. We are the same. If we have the practice, we can neutralize the toxic elements that enter us and transform garbage into flowers.

The skandhas play an important role in our continuation. And yet, we must also train ourselves to see that we go into the future *beyond* the combination of the skandhas. We must see ourselves as a cluster, not a single element; a cluster of flowers, not a single flower. All of these—karma of thought, speech, and action—are us. We are the totality of our karma.

Working with Inputs and Outputs

PHÁP LƯU

In the previous section, Thầy uses the language of "inputs" and "outputs" to describe the functioning of karma. He explains that our karma—our output—depends in large part on what we take in through our six senses: eyes, ears, nose, tongue, body, and mind. This process isn't a mechanistic one; it is organic. And we have the capacity to intervene, both in terms of what we allow in through our senses and how we work with what does come in. We can help shape the current of our actions. This influence we have is a key feature of Thầy's teaching on continuation as we'll see in the pages and chapters to come.

Guarding our senses—being mindful of what we do or do not allow in—is a basic way to affect how we continue in the world. If we are new to mindfulness practice, we need to remove ourselves altogether from difficult situations. When a conversation becomes heated, or when we find ourselves watching a violent film as mentioned above, we can excuse ourselves and choose walking meditation outside instead. As our practice deepens, we're better equipped to handle unwholesome inputs. We notice what's coming in; we recognize that it can feed emotions like anger, hatred, and despair, and we practice bringing our attention back to our body and our breathing. By paying attention to something neutral or wholesome—like our breathing—we remove the necessary condition (our attention) that allows the unwholesome thought to arise. This is a strategy, grounded in mindful awareness, for intervening in the input-output process. It's what Thầy means by "neutralizing the toxic elements that enter us." We create wholesome karma even when what's coming in isn't so wholesome.

This is not just theory—we can use these insights to change our behavior. When we bring our attention to our breathing, when we ground ourselves in the body, we cut off the kind of thinking that makes violence, sensual desire, or hatred manifest in us and in the world. Please do try it for yourself.

P. L.

Karmic Effect

Karma can have two kinds of effect: immediate and delayed. For example, if you say something untrue, it affects you right away, but it also affects you later, after people discover that you've lied. You must face the consequences of that discovery. We know that things we do now can make us suffer ten or twenty years later.

When you have a thought of loving kindness, the world profits and so do you—the effect is immediate. When you say something nice to another person, you both benefit from that loving speech. If we know how to handle our thoughts, speech, and action, we will continue to create happiness in ourselves, each other, and the world, even when our body is no longer present in its current form.

A Beautiful Continuation in the Here and Now

I live my daily life in such a way that I can go beautifully into the world. I want to think beautiful thoughts of loving kindness, compassion, understanding, and love. And every time I have a thought, I offer myself to you—to my students, my friends, and the world. That is output; that is my continuation. I want to transform all negative inputs before I go into the cosmos, into my friends, and into my students.

You can also ensure a beautiful continuation. In the here and now, when you come back to yourself, you have the power to shape your continuation. Our continuation is not something in the future—it takes place in the present moment. Please act skillfully to ensure a good future for yourself and for future generations.

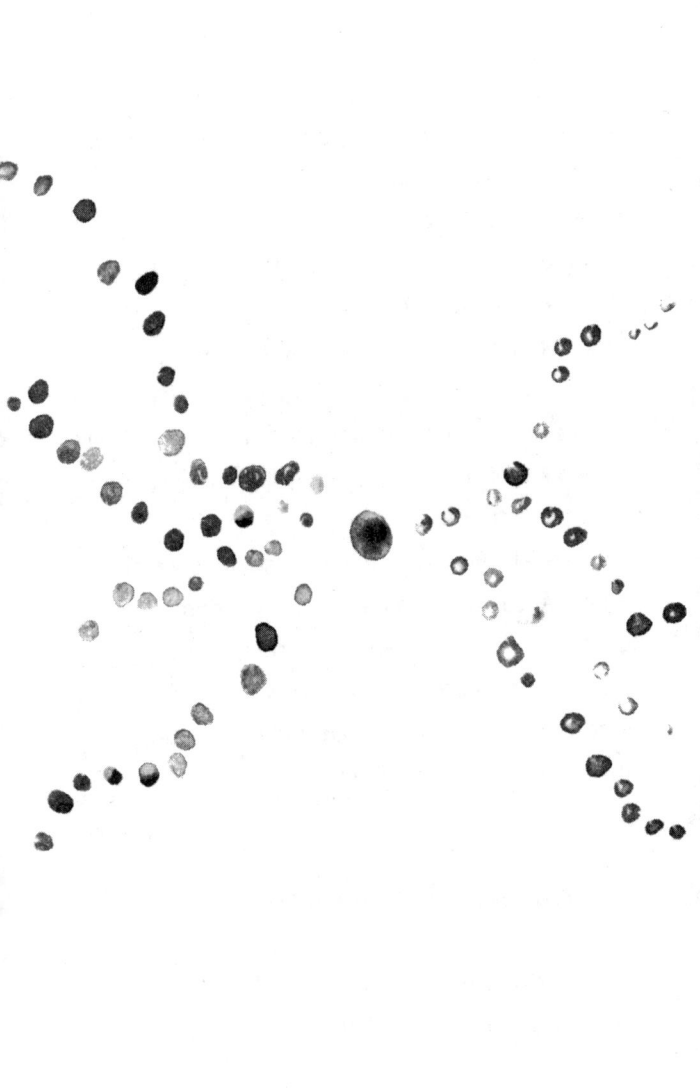

If you produced a thought yesterday that was not worthy of you, you can correct it today; you can transform that continuation. Free will is possible in the here and now. If you have Right View, you will be able to produce a different thought, a thought that carries within it understanding, compassion, and nondiscrimination. The moment you produce this wonderful thought, it will go out and catch the other thought that you produced yesterday. And in the space of half a second it will be able to transform that thought.

We always have the chance to correct the past. We say that the past is already gone, but the past is always returning in a new manifestation, and we can correct it if needed. Do something different today based on Right View and transform the whole situation. This is possible.

Karma and Right View

Right View is the foundation of all ethical action. When you have Right View, your thinking is Right

Thinking, your speech is Right Speech, and your action is Right Action. The path of well-being has to begin with Right View.

Right View is the foundation *and* fruit of our practice. Mindfulness leads to concentration and concentration leads to insight, or Right View. Right View is the view that transcends all views. It is free from discrimination, free from dualistic thinking. When we speak of Right View, we don't mean a view that's superior to all other kinds of views. As long as you're caught in one view, you can't have Right View. Instead, Right View is the absence of all views—for example, the views of birth, death, being, nonbeing, subject, and object—and it can remove all discrimination, intolerance, anger, fear, and despair.

Insight and Action

PHÁP LƯU

In the previous passage, Thầy notes that when we grasp onto any view, our entire experience becomes shaped and filtered by that way of seeing the world. We receive new inputs and information that might challenge the fixed view that we're trying to hold onto, but instead we may distort our perception of the new input to align with our established views—like the bark of a tree that grows around a nail which has been driven into it. Change happens, and yet we remain committed to our previous view. Right View—the letting go of all views—helps us learn, grow, develop, and act in a free and natural way, without the limiting influence of fixed opinions or beliefs, language structures, or deep-seated habits, whether personal, cultural, or ancestral.

It isn't easy to become aware of our hidden, deeply ingrained biases, let alone abandon them. This is our practice, though: not to be caught by any views, even Buddhist teachings. As Thầy makes clear in his description of Right View, we aren't replacing old established views with new fixed ones. To generate real insight, to see with unclouded eyes, takes diligence and courage—we need to feel at ease in the world living and working without any fixed conceptual scaffolding. From that place of clear looking, from Right View, our thinking, speech, and action naturally bring about well-being and understanding. Right View is the key to the entire Eightfold Path proposed by the Buddha.[2] It is the kind of insight that we will explore in the next chapter.

P. L.

---

2   The Eightfold Path (Right View, Right Thought, Right Speech, Right Action, Right Livelihood, Right Diligence, Right Mindfulness, and Right Concentration) is the path the Buddha described to overcome all our afflictions. It is the path of happiness that stops the kind of actions that create suffering.

2

Who Is Reborn?

Nonself: The Key to Freedom

PHÁP LƯU

THE SPIRIT OF OPENNESS and curiosity is the heart of Buddhist meditation. In this chapter, Thầy asks us to adopt that spirit as we consider the teachings on nonself. The Buddha had the insight that even though we tend to create a concept of a self, if we look deeply into our own experience in the world, we find nothing there to call a distinct "self" at all. We see that this body is always changing. We did not own it when we were born and we cannot hold onto it even while we are still alive, let alone when we die. As Thầy often taught us, our body is like a river. This is true as well for our feelings, our perceptions, our mental formations, and our consciousness. This observation is what the Buddha meant when he spoke about nonself. When we get the insight into the nonself nature of ourselves and all phenomena, we become free. This insight is the key to understanding rebirth and continuation at their deepest level.

If we really practice it, the teaching of nonself can lead to liberation. Yet it's important not to get caught in the idea of nonself. We should treat the Buddha's teachings as medicine, not as dogma. The teaching of nonself is a remedy for our attachment to our ideas about a self. If we go on and on to ourselves and others about nonself just for the sake of proving a theory about nonself, we're already trapped in the *concept* of nonself. We may find ourselves using the teaching of nonself as a hammer against those who find comfort in the belief in an enduring soul, a static self or identity. Rather, see the teaching of nonself as a medicine, something that we realize in our way of acting in every moment. Others will see our lightness, happiness, and joy, and become curious. They may want to know what makes us so.

Looking deeply into rebirth and continuation requires us to look deeply into what we think of as our self. To do this, we must rely on our direct observation of our experience. The medicine of nonself and interbeing—which we'll learn more about below—helps us remove unnecessary notions that complicate and obscure our view of reality. Looking closely at our own experience, we see reality for what it is, and we establish a right view—a clear view—which is free from all concepts, ideas, and notions.

P. L.

Nonself and Rebirth

The vast majority of Buddhists believe in rebirth or reincarnation. However, their belief is based on what we consider to be a wrong view of the self. They believe that there is a self or a soul distinct from the body, and when the body is gone, the soul survives and seeks another body to enter and continue. That is one teaching of rebirth, but it isn't the deep teaching of the Buddha.

We must avoid falling into the concepts of continuation and rebirth based on the attachment to a self. Understanding continuation and rebirth without letting go of the idea of a separate self is a very superficial level of Buddhism. The Buddha's deep teaching on continuation is based on the insight reflected in the three Dharma seals: nonself, impermanence, and nirvana.[3]

---

3 Thầy says, "Any teaching that does not bear the marks of [the three Dharma seals]... cannot be conceived to be an authentic teaching of the Buddha. The three Dharma seals should not be looked upon like a description of reality only. They should be looked upon as instruments we can use to train ourselves in looking and in seeing things."

Even though there is action, retribution, and rebirth,[4] this doesn't mean we need a "self." Just as water can be reborn as ice, ice can be reborn as clouds, and clouds can be reborn as a river. There is continuation, but there is no need for an unchanging, undying self to be reborn. If you plant corn, you get corn; if you plant beans, you get beans. That is true, but no self is needed. When all the conditions are sufficient, the seed of corn becomes a plant of corn, and there will be corn, but a self isn't required for that to happen.

The first of the *Paramārtha Gāthā*s of Asanga is "There is absolutely no subject, no actor, and no one who receives the fruit of action. Phenomena have no function."[5] This is amazing. The first sentence says that there is absolutely no subject—no

---

4 Retribution here means the effects of our actions. It doesn't have a sense of punishment or vengeance. It could be positive, neutral, or negative, or a mix of these. These effects come in the form of our five skandhas as well as our environment.

5 Asanga was a monk, a systematizer of Buddhist teachings, and one of the most prominent proponents of Manifestation-Only teachings (*Vijñaptimātratā-vāda*). His *Yogācārabhūmi-Śāstra*, which contains the Paramārtha Gāthās, is a major compendium and source text for teachings on Buddhist psychology.

boss, no actor, no receiver, no performer of action, and no receiver of the fruit of action. Nonetheless, when conditions are sufficient, there is action. When those conditions cease, action ceases. There is no self involved.

Nonself is the cream, the essence of the Buddha's teaching. There are millions of Buddhists in the world, but those who can see and understand this teaching are very few. Most Buddhists are devotees whose understanding is still caught in the notion of a separate self. To truly understand the Buddha's teachings, we must realize the reality of nonself. Gradually, with practice, as our understanding of Buddhism deepens, we will be able to let go of the idea of a self, a soul, and all the superstitions that go along with these concepts.

Banyan Trees

In Asia, there is a commonly known tree called the banyan tree, which has a complex system of roots and many branches.

Aerial roots grow down from the branches and find their way to the ground, where they take root. Gradually, they grow larger to become almost like a second, a third, a fourth tree. They also bring nutrients from the ground up to nourish the main trunk and the original branches. Each of these trunks has roots in the ground.

Looking at it from one perspective, we may see seven, eight, or more trees, but in fact, there are not seven different trees. Saying that there is one tree is also incorrect. They are not one, but they are not seven either. We see very clearly that six or more of the trees are the continuation of the first tree. Suppose part of the first tree rots, and the tree is cut at the trunk. When the first tree is cut, we consider it to be dead, no longer existing. But the other six trees have grown, and the first tree continues to exist in these new forms. We might think there is death, but there really isn't. There is only continuation.

The correct understanding of continuation and rebirth according to Buddhist teachings must be based on the truth of no birth, no death, no self, not one, not many, no coming, and no going. The image of the banyan tree can help us see the nonself nature of our five skandhas and let go of attachment to any particular one.

A Bamboo Grove

The image of a bamboo grove also helps us understand continuation and rebirth on the basis of nonself. A bamboo grove may seem to have many separate bamboo trees growing, but when we look deeply, we see that a mass of roots underneath the ground connects them all. For example, we may see a new bamboo shoot sprouting from a mass of bamboo roots. If we look superficially, we might think this new bamboo shoot is different from the other ones. But in reality, they all share the same nature. And looking deeply beneath the surface, we see the nonself nature of the bamboo.

If someone comes and cuts down one shoot, we might think there is death. But in reality life continues. That shoot might sprout in another place later on. Although they are not exactly the same, one shoot is not entirely different from another one either. If it cannot grow in one place, it will grow elsewhere. These images help us see more clearly the teachings of the Buddha on continuation and rebirth.

The Roots of Self

PHÁP LƯU

These images of the banyan tree and the bamboo grove help us to see continuation in light of nonself. But where does our strong sense of a separate self come from in the first place?

Thầy often taught us how to realize the illusion of our separateness. A helpful starting point is to recognize the root of our sense of separation, which in part lies in our survival instinct—what's called, in Buddhist psychology, our *jīvitindriya*. This instinct, or faculty of life, plays a natural evolutionary function in living beings, and it also contributes to our tendency to cling to life out of a fear of death. This survival instinct and its tendency to grasp at what it believes will sustain it becomes the basis for a belief in self and allows for our illusion of separateness to take hold.

Because of this strong sense of self, when we learn about nonself, we think there's something—ego, self—to destroy or get rid of. But that's incorrect. A better way to overcome our attachment to a self is to *stop feeding* the notion of separateness in our thinking. If a plant has deep and tenacious roots, we can't just cover it up with a tarp, cut its stem, or tear off some of its branches and expect it to wither away completely. It will likely have enough resources to continue growing. We must instead cut off nourishment at the root. Likewise, we need to remove the source of nourishment that feeds our belief in a separate self. Only then will that belief cease to entangle us.

Our fear of dying born from our survival instinct nourishes our belief in a separate self. When we touch the insight of no birth and no death—when we touch Right View—our fear of dying lessens and our clinging to life eases. That self we've created no longer has a strong basis to arise. Thầy's examples of the banyan tree and the bamboo grove help us to look deeper to observe the ways in which contin- uation is always going on. And as our fear is allayed, understanding grows. We can recog- nize and smile to our idea of a self—that edifice within ourselves. Our attachment to it is no longer as strong as it once was.

I've found that it doesn't work to try to "destroy" our ego or sense of self. The root giving rise to that wrong view is still there. We should instead learn to stop nourishing the root by making a change in how we live each moment.

The preferences—likes and dislikes—we

attach ourselves to play a big role in how we get caught in a notion of self. As we grow and experience life's joys and hardships, we find ourselves trying to control and curate our experience of life. We develop ways of thinking and acting based on a desire for more happiness and less suffering, and we habituate ourselves to look at happiness and suffering as two separate things. This dualism frames our way of looking at the world. Meditation is a concrete way to keep our mind open and let go of this dualistic way of thinking. If we stop and come back to our breathing, we can open our mind again and again to the raw experience of the present moment. That experience transcends all notions of good, bad, desirable or distasteful. Looking deeply with mindfulness, we can see for ourselves how a comparing mind—always looking to win, be number one, or find the best or the perfect—leads to more suffering. When we compare life and death, thinking that life is good and death is bad, our fear of death and our survival instinct become ever more activated; we cling to life, we struggle, and we suffer. But as we start to discover that death is in life, that life is in death—that one cannot be without the other and that both happen in every moment—we learn to let go. We can choose to nourish openness in every moment. This is freedom.

P. L.

Impermanence: Birth and Death in Every Moment

At first, you may believe in a self or a soul that always remains the same. But in reality, there is nothing that can remain the same in two consecutive moments. "You" of this moment is no longer the "you" of the previous moment. We cannot see this if we have not gone deep enough and touched the true nature of no birth and no death, no self and no other, no being and no nonbeing.

Impermanence of Body

Things exist only in one *kṣana*,[6] one millisecond; this is also true of our body. Cells die in order to give rise to other cells. In a month, many of our cells will be renewed. It's like a river. You cannot swim twice in the same river. Even though the name stays the same, the water in it is totally new. And it's not the same person who enters the river tomorrow; you have changed already.

The question, "Where will we go when we die?" can be answered like this: if you know where you are going in this moment, you know where you go after you die. You are dying and being reborn right here and right now. We know that there are many cells in the body dying all the time to make room for other cells to be born. You don't need to arrive at some later point in order to die because birth and death are happening in the present moment.

---

6 *Kṣana* (pronounced kshana) is a Buddhist term for a fraction of a second.

Impermanence of Consciousness

Many philosophers and scientists alike have claimed that consciousness has a cinematographic nature. When we project a film, it appears to be something continuous and long-lasting. But we know that the film consists of separate pictures that last only a fraction of a second. Consciousness is like that; it's only a flash, lasting just one millisecond. And because moments of consciousness succeed each other continuously, we have the impression that consciousness is something long-lasting. In fact, the permanent nature of consciousness is just an illusion.

It's like a flame on the tip of a candle. You think that the flame is the same flame as a moment before, but that's not true. There's a succession of many flames, one after another, that give the impression of a fixed identity. The flame of this moment gives rise to the flame of the next moment. And the flame of the next moment gives rise to the flame of the following moment.

In Buddhism, there is another beautiful illustration of this. At night, someone holds a torch and draws a circle in the air with it in the dark. If they are doing the movement quickly and you are standing at a distance, you have the impression that there is a circle of fire. But, in fact, there is only a succession of points of flame. The circle of fire is only an optical illusion. Permanence is an illusion, and the basic mistake is to believe that we have a consciousness, or a soul, that is always the same. Everything is impermanent.

Mentally and physically, you are of a cinematographic nature; you are reborn in every instant. You are renewed in every instant to become a new person, a new being. And if you know how to do it, your renewal is beautiful. With karma, you can assure a better, more beautiful continuation. If you know how to handle your thinking, your speech, and your actions, you will become more beautiful. The fact is that you don't need to wait until you die in order to see what happens to you. Look in the present moment and see that birth and death are going on in you at every moment, both in your body and in your consciousness.

No Stable Actor

PHÁP LƯU

We tend to think, when a person does something, that the person and the action are separate from one another. And we think that the person who produces the action will continue unchanged into the future and experience the fruit of that action—that the initial actor and the later experiencer of the effects are one and the same. But in the teachings above on nonself and impermanence, Thầy shows us why this turns out to be a wrong view—the idea of a separate, permanent actor who becomes the experiencer of the act cannot be observed in our actual experience.

Clinging to notions of a permanent actor and experiencer can obscure a deeper understanding of how we continue into the future. For example, when we light a matchstick, the flame that manifests consumes the carbon within the matchstick. No one would consider the charred remains of the matchstick to be the same as the matchstick prior to lighting. There is no stable "actor/experiencer" here. It would be a waste of time to treat the charred matchstick like an unlit one and try to get fire from it.

And yet, it's quite common to believe that we have an unchanging self, to believe that the person who produces an action isn't fundamentally changed by the action itself. We suffer when we struggle unsuccessfully to be the same person we were before some specific event: before the accident, before we had a child, before our partner passed away. If we get the insight that we are not the same person as the one who acted, we suffer less. We don't cling to the idea of a static identity continuing on through space and time. But as Thầy points out in the next section, it's not as simple as becoming another person altogether—looking with the eyes of signlessness, we see that we're neither the same as nor entirely different from who we were in the past.

P. L.

Impermanence, Not Annihilation

When you look through a family album, you may see a picture of yourself as a three-year-old child. Are you the same person as that little child? The answer is this: you are neither the same person nor a completely different one. You have grown up into an adult. Your form, feelings, mental formations, and perceptions are different. But you are not a completely different person either because you are a continuation of that child.

Many years ago during a retreat, I gave a kernel of corn to each child. I asked them to go home, plant it in a pot, and water it every day. Then, once the kernel had grown into a plant, the child could ask, "My dear plant of corn, do you remember when you were just a tiny little seed?" The plant of corn might respond, "Me? A little seed? I don't believe it!" I told the children that, if they were eloquent enough, they could convince the plant of corn that she was once a tiny kernel.

Looking skillfully, we'd see the kernel of corn

still there in the plant of corn. "Is the kernel still alive, or has it died?" is quite a deep question to ask a child. Yet it is possible even to teach children about no birth and no death, no being and no nonbeing.

In Buddhism, we talk about *signlessness*. Sign means form or appearance. Once a growing plant, the kernel of corn may no longer be recognizable as its sign, its original appearance, but that does not mean that it isn't there anymore. When we were conceived, we were also a little seed—much smaller than the kernel of corn. That seed became a little child, but where is that little child now? Are they still alive? When those of us who practice meditation look at the plant of corn, we can still see the kernel. It is there, alive, although it doesn't appear in its familiar form. Do you think that the little child in you has died, or do they continue in you? Do you talk to them, or are you too busy?

We may think that if the grain does not die, the birth of a plant is not possible. But is it true that something must die for something else to be born? When a cloud becomes rain, is something dying or not? Is something being born or not? The death of a cloud means the birth of the rain. If the birth of the rain is not there, the death of the cloud is not possible. Birth and death are the two sides of the same coin—you cannot pull them apart.

In the word signlessness, *sign* means the appearance, the form, the object of our perception. A cloud has its own form or appearance. And thanks to that appearance, we recognize it as a cloud. The appearance of the rain is different from the appearance of the cloud. But, as the Buddha says, where there is perception, there is deception. If we are caught by the sign or the appearance of something, we are fooled; we cannot see the truth.

If a cloud cannot die, then our loved ones cannot die either. With our normal way of looking, we think that our grandmother, our grandfather, our ancestors have died. But when we look with the eyes of signlessness, we see that they are still alive in every cell of our body. We can talk to our grandfather, to our grandmother, right in this very moment—they will hear us.

Practicing signlessness is the way to touch

reality. If you are not caught in the sign, you can have a correct perception of reality. If the child has the eyes of signlessness, they can see the kernel of corn in the plant of corn. Whether we succeed in our contemplation on birth and death depends on whether we can see things with the eyes of signlessness.

Transcending Notions, Touching Nirvana

The Flame Continues

Let us consider a flame. Before it manifests as a flame, you cannot say that it does not exist, or that it belongs to the realm of nonbeing. And when it manifests as a flame, you cannot say that it now belongs to the realm of being either. It cannot be described in terms of being or nonbeing.

Before we light the match, we can say to the flame, "My dear little flame, I know you are there somewhere. Manifest for us." And the flame says,

"Dear Thầy, I am ready to manifest for you. All conditions seem to be sufficient, except the last one." The match is there, the matchbox is there, oxygen is there, and when we provide the flame with the final necessary condition—striking the match—she manifests beautifully. Now if I ask the flame, "My dear little flame, where have you come from?" The flame will respond: "Dear Thầy, I have not come from anywhere. My true nature is no coming. I have not come from the North, the South, the East, or the West. When conditions are sufficient, I manifest." After blowing the flame out, we may ask, "Dear little flame, we miss you. Where have you gone?" And the flame will answer, "Dear Thầy, I have not gone anywhere. I do not go to the north, south, east, or west. When conditions are no longer sufficient, I stop manifesting in this form in order to manifest in other forms. Heat, smoke, and ash are my new manifestations."

For a few seconds, the flame creates a beautiful image that penetrates into all of us. It creates heat that enters the cosmos. It creates some particulates and gas that go up to become a cloud of

smoke. During her brief manifestation, we can say that the flame produces actions and continues in us and around us. Nothing is lost; the flame does not die. For those of us who know how to meditate, we see clearly that the flame always continues.

Our true nature is the same as that of the cloud and the flame: the nature of no birth and no death, no being and no nonbeing, no coming and no going. The ultimate truth transcends all kinds of notions, including notions of being and nonbeing, birth and death, coming and going. If you don't let go of these notions, you can never touch the ultimate.

Nirvana in the Present Moment

The ultimate is nirvana. Nirvana is the extinction of suffering and afflictions, and this is possible only when we can extinguish notions like birth and death, being and nonbeing. We can define nirvana in very clear terms: it is the absence of all notions. Suffering is born from notions, and so nirvana is the absence of suffering.

Nirvana is available right in the here and now. Suppose you are walking barefoot, accidentally step on a briar, and get some thorns in your foot. Immediately you lose all peace and happiness. As soon as you remove one thorn, you get some relief. And the more thorns you remove, the greater the relief and peace. In the same way, the removal of our afflictions—our anger, fear, and despair—is the presence of nirvana. As soon as we begin to remove our afflictions, we start to experience nirvana.

Some people think that when you touch nirvana, you don't have to be reborn anymore, that you are freed from the rounds of birth and death; you now belong to the realm of nonbeing. But that view is very misleading. Even some Western scholars of Buddhism hold this wrong view. They believe that the aim of Buddhism is to achieve a kind of eternal death, or eternal nonbeing. But our aim as practitioners is not to reach a state of annihilation. The Buddha's view is a kind of insight that transcends both the notion of total annihilation and the notion of eternal life. Through meditation, we can remove these kinds of notions so that we have Right View. Once you remove these and other pairs of notions—birth and death, being and nonbeing, self and other—you have peace, you have nirvana, and you don't worry anymore.

Practicing Nonself

Nonself is not a philosophy to study but a daily practice. The experience of nonself heals our loneliness, grief, and despair. In the monastery, we practice nonself as we listen to the bell, sit in meditation, practice walking meditation, or chant together. Before a period of sitting meditation begins, our mind might be dispersed, but when the bell is invited to begin the sitting, everyone stops, returns to their breath, and breathes in unison. That collective energy permeates each person. I breathe for you, you breathe for me. You breathe for her and she breathes for you. All separate individuals breathe as one body, become one body, breathing together beautifully.

Similarly, when we practice walking meditation correctly, we are no longer like a drop of oil floating in a bowl of water. We are no longer a separate self. Walking together, we become one body, we become a river. With the insight of nonself, we walk with immense happiness. Suffering, worries, separateness, and individual concerns vanish. Just as when we hear the sound of the bell, the energy of mindfulness arises and connects us as we walk, naturally transforming us from isolated individuals into a collective Sangha body.

Chanting is another practice like this. In Buddhism, we chant not to pray but to realize that the so-called "I am" is no longer there. Everyone participating in the chanting must act as one; the one chanting and the one listening to the chanting are not two. The chanter is the listener, and the listener is the chanter. Once we enter this experience, all feelings of inferiority, superiority, or equality cease,[7] and we no longer suffer.

---

7 Whenever we compare ourselves to others—that we are better, worse, or the same as them—suffering follows. Freedom from comparing leads to happiness right away.

Mindfulness practice has many dimensions. We should not content ourselves with a shallow dimension but, with practice, should gradually go deeper. When walking, we must walk for our whole community, for our father, our mother, our spiritual and blood ancestors, and for those who suffer around the world. Only by walking like this can we truly see our many bodies. In this way, we can live with the wisdom of the Buddha and the wise ones in this very life.

Experiencing Nonself in Daily Life

PHÁP LƯU

Thầy often led us in what I find to be a particularly powerful practice of nonself: the practice of walking with our ancestors. I know that my parents held my hand when I took my first steps, cheering me on as I walked upright on the earth. And with a deep understanding of continuation, I can see them with me now. We walk together in a very real way; it is with the feet of my mother and father that I now take my own steps. They are present in every cell in my body. This practice is available to me at any moment.

Our mother and father may never have had the chance to walk mindfully on earth, so we can take mindful steps for them. I even like to speak to my parents directly as I walk. "Mom, I know you're there, I know you're running. You ran your whole life to make me breakfast, to get me off to school, to make sure my lunch was packed." By walking mindfully, I help transform my mom's worry and anxiety with each solid step I take on the earth. I can heal the past right in the present moment.

This isn't just a nice idea—it's very real, very practical. The tendency to rush, to be distracted, to worry, to get angry—things that may have haunted our parents throughout their lives—are also carried in every cell of our bodies. "Dad, I handed you the screwdrivers when you were working under the car to change the oil. I was there when you got angry because the dog chewed on the screwdrivers we put in the garage." I carry my dad's anger within me, so I practice to transform it. With each step I take, I come back to the earth, I send our anger into the earth, and I let it go. This is a concrete practice of nonself.

When we're together with others, perhaps at a work meeting, we can look around the room and see ten or twelve other people. Looking with the eyes of nonself, we can see many, many more of us seated around the room. All our ancestors are also there, from many generations back and from all over the world. In the United States, for instance, many of us have ancestors who came to escape situations of poverty in their home country or were forced to come here through the slave trade. The suffering and the joys of these many people are carried by those seated with us in our work meeting. Right there, sitting with our colleagues, we can experience a global summit of all our ancestors. It is possible to realize non-self, to see continuation and rebirth, right in the most common experiences of our daily lives.

P. L.

3

Our Many Bodies

PHÁP LƯU

AS WE SAW in chapter two, the subtle ways that we grasp onto abstractions and ideologies create suffering. One of the concepts we tend to hold most tightly is our concept of the body. We think, "This is my body. This layer of skin is the boundary—everything within and beneath it is me, and everything beyond it isn't." In chapter three, Thầy helps us understand that this view of our body is only a persistent habit of mind. Our body's true nature is much deeper and vaster.

Science also offers a more expansive view of who we are than what our habits of mind suggest. We know that without the oxygen we breathe or the water and food we ingest, we wouldn't have a body at all. All kinds of particles move through our body at all times. The very atoms that make up our bodies are constantly replaced and recycled. While it may seem like the atoms that compose our bodies are immutable, even they have changed and evolved since the Big Bang, through fusion in stars and supernova explosions. We come from everywhere, and from time immemorial, composed of an everchanging cast of atomic characters.

So, when we look deeply, we realize that the body is far more complex and mysterious than we typically assume. Thầy offers a fresh perspective from which to see the interbeing nature of our body. Interbeing means that we cannot be by ourselves alone; we can only inter-be with all phenomena within and around us—with the entire cosmos. If we remove the sun, the air, the water, the trees, the plants that allow us to live, we remove ourselves as well. With this insight, we see that the entire cosmos is represented within our body.

Thầy gives the teachings that follow on our many bodies to wake us up from our very limited understanding of where and what our body is—to touch this interbeing nature. It helps us to realize that what we consider to be inside the body is simply a concept, one that co-arises with our concept of "outside the body."

Contemplating this deep teaching, we begin to understand better the true weight and far reach of our actions of body, speech, and mind. We are so much more than who we think we are; our effect in the world is expansive. This insight can offer motivation to consider the broad effects, both in space and time, of all that we do; to create kind thoughts, speech, and actions; and to bring happiness to ourselves and the world.

P. L.

Human Body

Recognizing our body as a wonderful manifestation of interbeing is very different from how we normally think about our body. There is no separate body that is a lone entity, and yet we are very much inclined to think that there is. As humans, we are made exclusively of nonhuman elements. Human beings cannot exist by themselves alone; we have to inter-be with animals, plants, and minerals. If we remove all these nonhuman elements, there's no humanity left.

Our human body is a wonder, and we know that we should consume in such a way that promotes physical health and well-being. But when we spend hours in front of our computer, lost in work, we may forget that we have a body at all. And when body and mind are not together, we are not truly alive. The mind needs to be embodied in order to be a real mind; the body needs to be inhabited by the mind in order to be a living body.

The Buddha was, first of all, a human being with a human body. Therefore, to awaken like the

Buddha, we need a physical body. Master Linji[8] said that the human being and Buddha always go together; you cannot take the Buddha out of the human being and you cannot take the human being out of the Buddha. All of us have a human body, so all of us can become a buddha. This is good news.

Buddha Body

Every one of us possesses a Buddha body, and though our Buddha body has not yet fully manifested, it exists in the form of seeds. "Buddha" means awakening, great understanding, and great love, and we already carry the seeds of awakening, love, and understanding within us. Yet, in daily life, worries, anger, and sorrows prevent the Buddha body within us from growing and fully manifesting. We have the capacity to love, the capacity

---

8 Linji (d. 866 CE) was a monk and teacher from China central and foundational to a major lineage (the Linji tradition) of the Chan (or Meditation) School. The Plum Village tradition is in the Linji lineage.

for mindfulness and great understanding, but because these capacities are not properly nurtured, they have not yet grown strong.

We don't have to travel to look for our Buddha body; it's available right here and right now. We're all capable of drinking our tea mindfully. Every one of us can breathe, walk, and eat in mindfulness. Every one of us can speak and listen with compassion. When you are awake and fully present, when you can get in touch with the wonders of life, you are a buddha.

We should take care of our Buddha body and allow it to grow. As the Buddha in us grows, our understanding and love grow with the Buddha body, and we become happier and freer. The Buddha body in us is not an abstract idea; it is something very real and concrete. All of us have the capacity to understand and to love. There's no reason not to believe in our Buddha body.

Dharma Body

The Practice of Mindfulness, Concentration, and Insight

Besides having a Buddha body, we also have a Dharma body. In order to nourish the Buddha body in us, we have to practice. The practice of mindfulness, concentration, and insight is called the practice of the Dharma. When we sit, we sit mindfully so that we can enjoy our sitting. When we walk, we walk mindfully so that we can enjoy every step. When we eat, we eat mindfully and with concentration so that we can enjoy every morsel of food. Every moment of our daily life can be joyful and happy, thanks to the practice of mindfulness. When we wash our dishes, if we know how to do it mindfully, we enjoy washing the dishes. We can smile and practice mindful breathing while doing the dishes so that it becomes a moment of peace. And when we practice breathing mindfully, walking mindfully, eating mindfully, washing the dishes mindfully, the Buddha body in us grows. The practice of mindfulness, the practice of the Dharma, helps our Buddha body to grow.

A Buddha is made of mindfulness, concentration, and insight, and these three energies are generated by the practice of the Dharma. As a friend of the Buddha—if you practice mindful breathing, mindful walking, mindful eating, mindful dishwashing—you have a Dharma body.

When we have a strong practice, our Dharma body is solid, and our Buddha body grows very quickly. We carry that Dharma body with us always. Wherever you go—to the supermarket, to the bus stop—you bring the Dharma body with you.

The Buddha's Teachings

The term "Dharma body" refers to our practice, and it also refers to the Buddha's teachings themselves. In the past, a monk named Vakkali was deeply enamored of the Buddha's physical appearance. He would follow the Buddha closely, captivated by his beauty, but he neglected to listen deeply to the Buddha's Dharma talks. The Buddha eventually reproached Vakkali and dismissed him from his role as the Buddha's attendant in order to help Vakkali overcome his attachment. Vakkali was deeply distressed, but over time, he transformed himself and practiced diligently. When Vakkali fell gravely ill, the Buddha visited him and asked

—Vakkali, are you in pain?
—Yes, Blessed One, I am in great pain and close to death.

—Have you been practicing?
—Yes, I have been practicing.

—Do you have any regrets?
—No, I have no regrets, except that I can no longer follow you and behold your form daily.

The Buddha said
—Vakkali, my physical form is impermanent, subject to birth and death. Do not cling to this form. If you are practicing diligently, you already possess my Dharma body,

which will endure forever. You should hold onto the Dharma body, not this physical body.

The physical body of the Buddha, of the teacher, disintegrates but the Dharma body does not. Once you have the Dharma body of the Buddha—the true teachings—there is no need to cling to the teacher.[9]

Sangha Body

You have a Buddha body, a Dharma body, and also a Sangha body. The Sangha is a group of people who come together in order to practice mindfulness. It's very easy to keep our practice alive in a Sangha. Since everyone is breathing mindfully, walking mindfully, eating mindfully, we

9 Thầy trained his students to continue the community he found-ed when he would no longer be present in his usual form. We look to see Thầy in his students—meaning our monastic and lay co-practitioners. In this way we overcome our tendency to cling to Thầy's physical form.

naturally do the same. Practicing together, the Sangha generates a collective energy of mindfulness and concentration that nourishes us and supports our practice. If we really want to practice, we will seek out a Sangha, a community of practitioners, to support us on our path. When we do this, in addition to a Buddha and Dharma body, we also have a Sangha body. The Sangha is not exactly outside of us; it is inside. A Sangha is the best kind of environment, one that guides you, nourishes you, and helps your Buddha body and Dharma body grow.

In my tradition, we treasure the Sangha body. Without the Sangha body, we're likely to abandon our practice. When a tiger leaves the mountain and goes to the lowland, it will most likely be caught by humans and killed. When a practitioner leaves their Sangha, they will lose their practice and their life as a practitioner dies, like the tiger who leaves the mountain. The Sangha is our mountain, where we don't risk abandoning the practice.

Our Sangha should be a true Sangha, one where all its members practice the Dharma. As we do walking meditation, we really make mindful steps. As we do sitting meditation, we really nourish ourselves. We know how to release the tension in our body, handle a feeling of pain and sorrow, and cultivate joy and happiness. In a good Sangha, the Dharma is the true Dharma—not the spoken or written Dharma but the living Dharma. When you breathe mindfully, when you sit mindfully, when you walk mindfully, you produce the living Dharma. And if the living Dharma is there, surely the Buddha is also there. Therefore, the true Sangha carries within herself the true Dharma and the true Buddha.

Body Outside the Body

The term *body outside the body* means that our body is there outside of our physical body. If we can see ourselves outside of ourselves, outside of this body, we begin to see our true body; we transcend notions like being and nonbeing, existing or not existing.

There may be inmates in a prison somewhere sitting in meditation, practicing walking meditation, or smiling gently. They, too, are my body because they have read my books and are putting the teachings into practice. They are continuing my path. This is the body outside the body. Similarly, when a father looks at his child with the eyes of the Buddha, he will see that his child is also himself. He is the father, but he is also the child. Looking deeply, the father can recognize his body outside his own body. The child can also look at their father this way and recognize their body outside the body.

You are more than this body. To meditate is to see that you are everywhere; your nature is non-local.[10]

---

10 In light of general relativity and the continuum of spacetime, to realize our nature is non-local is also to realize it is non-temporal (i.e., outside of space and time).

Continuation Body

Whether your continuation body is beautiful or not depends on the quality of your thoughts, speech, and actions. When you look at these things, you see your continuation body very clearly. We have already seen that we are the sum of our three actions of body, speech, and mind. This is our karma, our continuation, and these actions continue into the future forever. We can never die.

We must be mindful in each moment of our daily life—the future depends on the present moment. But we don't need to wait until the complete disintegration of this body in order to begin to see our continuation body. It is possible for each of us to see our continuation right away. When a schoolteacher looks at their class, they can see their students as their continuation. If they are a happy schoolteacher, if they have a lot of freedom, compassion, and understanding, their students will also be happy and feel understood.

The cloud doesn't need to be transformed entirely into the rain in order to see her continuation body. The cloud looks down at the rain and sees herself in the rain. We should all practice to see our continuation body now. Then, when the time comes for the dissolution of our physical body, we will be able to release it easily.

Cosmic Body

Looking into your physical body, you can also recognize your cosmic body. If the cosmos is not there, your physical body cannot be here; your body would not be possible. The cosmos is the domain of all phenomena: the air, the water, the sun, the soil, and even the stars. Without the sunshine, for example, there would be no life on Earth, so you are made of sunshine. You are a child of the sun. And without food from the earth, you could not exist either. So you are also a child of the earth. Your little human body contains the whole cosmos.

I often refer to the sun as our second heart, a heart which lies outside our body but is as essential for our body as the heart inside our body. When the heart inside the body ceases to function, we know very well that we will die, but we often forget that if the heart outside our body, the sun, ceases to function, we will also die.

In the beginning we see things—phenomena—as existing outside of each other. But looking deeply, we see that things are interwoven with each other. You cannot take anything out of anything else. You cannot be by yourself, alone. You have to inter-be with the whole cosmos. A cloud, a pebble, a river, a star, everything obeys the law of interbeing.

True Nature of the Cosmos Body

Our eighth body is the "true nature of the cosmos" body. When we get in touch with everything that is—like the sunshine, vegetation, air, water, or stars—we touch the phenomenal world of appearances and signs. At the level of appearances, everything is changing, subject to birth and death, to being and nonbeing. But when we touch the phenomenal world deeply enough, we touch the true nature of the cosmos, the nature of no birth and no death, no coming and no going, no being and no nonbeing, and we transcend all these notions.

A wave on the ocean is subject to beginning and ending, to going up and coming down. The wave may be caught in the idea that "I am here now, and I will not be here later on." She may feel angry or afraid. But if the wave can go home to herself and touch her true nature—the water—her fear and anxiety will disappear. We, too, can touch our true nature of no birth and no death, no being and no nonbeing. Like the wave who realizes she is the water, we can experience absolute freedom and non-fear.

Contemplating Our Many Bodies

If you look deeply at your body, you can see your parents, your grandparents, all your ancestors, and the whole history of life on Earth. We see that our body is a formation, a composite made of everything else that we do not normally think of as body. You can see the sun, the moon and the stars, time and space. In fact, the whole universe has come together to form our body. Only one thing is missing from our body, and that is a *separate self*, a *separate existence*. If we put the sunlight back in the sun, the rain back in the clouds, and the minerals back in the earth, how could our body exist? All phenomena contain the whole universe. We can look at our body in such a way that we see its dependence on all things and thus see that it has no reality as a separately existing entity. You may like to take a moment now to do this, breathing in and out mindfully, as you read the following contemplation:

This body has been there for a long time, for millions of years. It is the continuation of many generations. It has never died.

I cannot take this body lightly. It is not mine alone. I cannot underestimate this body. It is the body of all my ancestors.

The mind is in this body. The mind gives rise to this body and this body gives rise to the mind. In this body, all the wonders of the life of the cosmos are to be found. The realm of no birth and no death, the Pure Land, and the Kingdom of God are also in this body. I cannot take it lightly. It contains all the mysteries of the cosmos.

This body is also a wonderful flower of the cosmos. I want to take good care of it. I want my body to reveal to me all the mysteries, all the wonders of the cosmos.

This body will be continued in many other forms, whether I have children and grandchildren or not. I want this body to continue beautifully for many lives to come.

Our Many Bodies: Generating Insight, Overcoming Anxiety

PHÁP LƯU

As we grow from an infant to a child, we develop a sense of where our body begins and ends. We have the experience, for instance, of moving our hand, our fingers, or any other part of our body by means of our nervous and musculoskeletal system—and we notice that there are other things in our field of vision, say a tree branch across the yard, that we cannot control or move in the same way. To move it we need to walk over and grab it with our hands. We think: "My hand is part of my body; the tree branch is not." We move from that experience to an idea that we are completely cut off and separate from that tree branch. Our angst, our existential anxiety and fear of death, come from this insistence that we are a separate body, a separate self.

Thầy's teaching in this chapter helps us get unstuck from this way of being in the world.

His challenge to our idea of a body as a separate entity helps us to remove obstacles that keep us from realizing our interbeing nature. Through these teachings, we can expand our understanding and see how that tree, for example, is a very real extension of our body: it takes in carbon dioxide and puts out oxygen that we breathe. It provides shade on a cool day. The paper that comes from trees that this book is written on—for those of us reading the physical book—brings you the words that help guide and transform your mind. We interare with the trees.

Nowadays, we may also contemplate the boundaries of our bodies when it comes to human-computer interfaces. As the internet and now AI have become extensions of how human beings communicate with and understand the world, social media profiles, avatars, and augmented reality interfaces are examples of how physical and digital forms of embodiment and identity intersect. In this chapter, Thầy helps us to see that extending the bounds of who we think we are is, in fact, nothing new. From a spiritual perspective, our body has never been limited to just this human form. It has always extended in many directions, temporally and spatially.

Historically, it's actually quite novel for us to think of this body as separate and only ours. For much of our species' existence, there wasn't sovereignty over the body in the way we understand it today. One's body was part of the community or family body; it included the rights, opinions, speech, and actions of one's children and parents. The body has traditionally been much more than just what's contained within this layer of skin.

When we see that we are not separate—from animals, plants, minerals, ancestors, descendants, and so forth—we become less fixated on what happens to this human body. We see our body like a leaf on the grand tree of our planet's ecosystem; we begin to operate from a vaster perspective. When a leaf falls, we don't hold a funeral for it—the leaf goes back to the soil and becomes rich humus for the growth of the tree. That kind of cyclic dance has gone on since long before humans were on this planet and will continue far into the future. This is the way of seeing, the Right View, that can heal our existential anxiety.

P. L.

4

Store Consciousness, Ripening, and Rebirth

PHÁP LƯU

IF WE UNDERSTAND how our mind works, we understand rebirth. Cause and effect, inputs and outputs, are directly observable—intimately, moment by moment—at the level of our own thinking. But we must truly see the process—what feeds our thinking, how thinking leads to action, and how these actions impact the seeds in our consciousness. When we do see what's happening, we see that there's only continuation—even at the level of our mind, there's no coming from nonbeing into being or vice versa. And there's no self running the show behind these mental processes. Everything that manifests in our mind does so from causes and conditions as part of an ongoing cycle.

In Manifestation-Only Buddhism we talk about this ripening process as store consciousness (ālāyavijñāna). This process goes on at an individual and collective level since beginningless time; it is in the very fabric of things as they are. We can think—as Thầy invites us—of the crust of the Earth, within which manifest and have manifested so many wondrous creatures, minerals, plants, and so forth. We are a part of that manifestation. Our ways of acting in the present moment affect how we and others will manifest in the future. The current climate crisis makes this process obvious. When we let go of ideas like internal and external with regard to consciousness, we begin to see this organic process of storage and ripening all around us. In the following chapter, Thầy helps us to understand more deeply the nature of store consciousness and the role it plays in the process of continuation.

P. L.

Three Aspects of Store Consciousness

Store consciousness has three aspects. The first is storing and preserving all the seeds (*bija*) of our experiences. The seeds buried in our store consciousness represent everything we have ever done, experienced, or perceived. Store consciousness draws together all these seeds just as a magnet attracts particles of iron. Maintaining all the seeds, keeping them alive so that they are available to manifest, is the most basic function of store consciousness.

The second aspect of store consciousness is the seeds themselves. A museum is more than the building, it is also the works of art that are displayed there. In the same way, store consciousness is not just the "storehouse" of the seeds but also the seeds themselves. The seeds can be distinguished from the store consciousness, but they can be found only in the storehouse. When you have a basket of apples, the apples can be distinguished from the basket. If the basket were empty, you would not call it a basket of apples. Store consciousness is, at the same time, both the storehouse and the content that is stored.

Seeds and Karma

The third aspect of store consciousness is ripening and perpetuation. Seeds give phenomena the ability to perpetuate themselves. If you plant a seed in springtime, by autumn a plant will mature and bear flowers. From those flowers, new seeds will fall to the earth, where they will be stored until they sprout and produce new flowers. Our mind is a field in which every kind of seed is sown—seeds of compassion, joy, and hope; seeds of sorrow, fear, and difficulties. Every day our karma—thoughts, words, and physical actions—plant new seeds in the field of our consciousness, and what these seeds generate becomes the substance of our life.

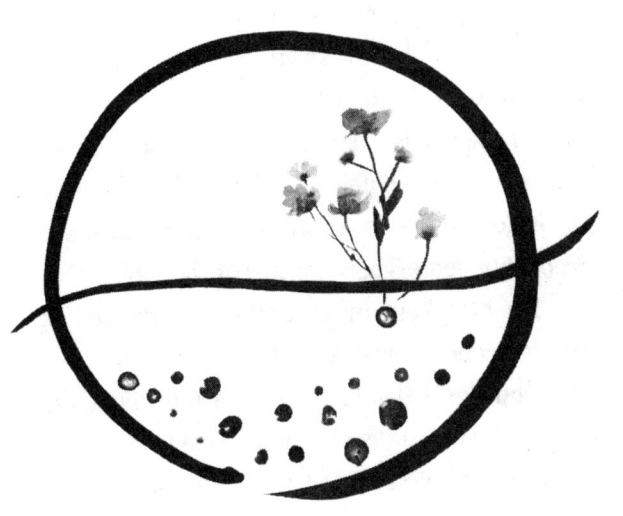

As we have seen, each of us is the sum of our actions. These actions are both the cause and result of seeds in our store consciousness. When we do something, our action is a cause. When it bears a result, it is an effect. Every act we make through our body, speech, and mind sows seeds in our consciousness, and our store consciousness preserves and maintains these seeds. In turn, the quality of the seeds in our store consciousness affects our actions of body, speech, and mind.

Our body, our mind, and the world are all manifestations of the seeds that are stored in our consciousness. Before something manifests, we usually say that it doesn't exist. Once we are able to perceive it, we say that it exists. But even though a phenomenon is unmanifested, it is always there, as a seed in our consciousness. All of our actions, experiences, and perceptions become seeds in our store consciousness, and even though we may think we have forgotten something, noth-ing that the store consciousness receives is lost; everything is stored there, unmanifested, until the conditions for its manifestation are present.

Transmitted Seeds

Some seeds are received by us during our lifetime, in the sphere of our experience. Some seeds, however, are innate—they were already present when we were born. At the time of our birth, seeds of suffering and happiness that were transmitted to us by many generations of our ancestors are already there. Many of our abilities, mannerisms, and physical features, as well as our values, were handed down to us by them. During our lifetime, when the conditions for their manifestation are favorable, some of these seeds will manifest. Some will not manifest in our own lifetime, but we will transmit them to our children, who will then transmit them on to their children. Perhaps a few generations later, during the lifetime of one of our great-grandchildren, the conditions will be favorable and certain of those transmitted seeds will then manifest.

The Emptiness of Transmission

To understand how the seeds in our store consciousness are transmitted across generations, the Buddha proposed looking into the transmission of the physical body. Your body has been transmitted to you by your father, your mother, and your ancestors; you have received this transmission; and your body is the object of this transmission. The three elements in this process of transmission are: the one who transmits, the object transmitted, and the recipient of the transmission.

The Buddha invites us to look into the nature of each thing and find the emptiness of transmission.[11] We ask ourselves the question, "What did my father transmit to me?" The answer is: He transmitted himself to me. The object transmitted is nothing other than himself, and I really am the continuation of my father. I am my father. Our ancestors are in us. Sometimes they manifest in the way we smile, speak, or think. Then we ask,

---

11 Emptiness of transmission means that the transmission is empty of a separate self.

"Who is the recipient of the transmission? Is it a separate entity?" No. The recipient of the transmission is the object of both the transmission and of the transmitter. The object of transmission is one with the transmitter.

Transmission and Agency

PHÁP LƯU

As Thầy explains above, the intergenerational transmission of seeds plays a vital role in our continuation. There are causes and conditions for everything, including the qualities that we take to be integral to who we are. These include the intergenerational trauma we inherit, but also our joy, heroism, deep aspirations, courage to help others, and altruism. All of this can come from our parents, teachers, friends, and the environment in which we were raised, and it exerts an influence on how we develop. The seeds that are transmitted to us may strongly influence who we become and how we continue in the world.

We often view who we are, including these qualities, from the perspective of a separate self. We tend to draw a boundary and say, "This is me, and that is not me. I am me; I am not my parents or grandparents. I am not my teachers or my friends." The teaching on transmission helps us become free from this artificial boundary we create around who we think we are. It allows us to recognize the causes and conditions as they are, rather than how we imagine them from a self-centered perspective. Every action from our ancestors has "perfumed," or influenced, the seeds in our consciousness.

As Thầy explains, all the seeds in our consciousness are impermanent—they're always changing and growing. This is the evolving nature of store consciousness, a process which is very much influenced by our own actions and intentions. The strength of the seeds that we have depends on our ancestors and our environment, but it also depends significantly on our own actions. This is a very important point:

we can play an active role in what manifests in our own consciousness and the effect it has on the world around us.

We find ourselves amid this ancestral stream of seeds ripening in the present moment. Through our actions right now of body, speech, and mind we are contributing to how those seeds become stronger or weaker going into the future. That is our continuation, not only in this body-mind complex but also in those around us: our friends, our students, young people, and even elders. They too can be transformed by our actions. Those who receive our karma are our continuation.

Just by thinking, we change ourselves, our environment, and those around us. For example, when you go into a room and someone is thinking angry or hateful thoughts, it's uncomfortable to be around them, even if they don't say or do anything. At the same time, when someone is filled with love and compassion and has kind thoughts, you feel at ease around them. They don't have to say or do anything.

> Our thoughts don't need to manifest as speech or physical action to have a real effect in the world. Our thinking is a very real part of our continuation.

P. L.

Seeds Are Neither Individual Nor Collective

Our store consciousness includes both individual and collective consciousness. What a certain society considers beautiful, for example, is a creation of the collective consciousness of that society. You believe that you have your own notion of beauty, but if you look deeply you will see that it has been formed from the notions of many other people. Our enjoyment of food is the same. To me, pickled mustard greens are delicious. My ancestors ate them, and the seeds in my consciousness have the habit of enjoying them also. To you, pickled mustard greens may not be tasty at all. Tasty or awful, beautiful or ugly, depends on the seeds in our consciousness, both individual and collective.

No seed in our consciousness is one hundred percent innate or one hundred percent transmitted. No seed is purely individual or purely collective. If you are a good musician, the seed of that ability is often considered to be your individual trait. But if we look deeply, we can see its collective nature as well. You might have received this ability from your ancestors, from your teachers, or even from listening to music. The seed is yours, it exists in your store consciousness, but it has been sown there by the happiness and suffering, the abilities and weaknesses of everyone with whom you've been in contact.

In fact, the distinction between innate and transmitted seeds—between individual and collective—is artificial. These distinctions are established in order to help us better understand on an intellectual level seemingly opposite concepts so that we can work with them in our practice. When our practice matures, when we see the interbeing nature of everything, we no longer need these distinctions.

Ultimately, we need to transcend ideas of individual and collective. Everything contains both: the collective and the individual inter-are. The individual always has an effect on the collective, and the collective always has an effect on the individual. All seeds in our store consciousness have this dual nature, individual and collective. It is important to remember this when we practice cultivating wholesome seeds and not to water the unwholesome ones.

When we speak of collective consciousness, we tend to have some idea of a consciousness that pervades society, changing with the issues and fashions of the day. But the collective aspect of seeds in our consciousness also comes from our ancestors and from all those who have gone before us. The seeds in our consciousness contain the experiences, ideas, and perceptions of many people throughout space and time.

The Collective Flow of Conscious Experience

PHÁP LƯU

Carl Sagan famously requested that the Voyager 1 space probe, as it sped toward the outer limits of our solar system and beyond, turn its camera back to photograph the Earth. The resulting image—now known as the Pale Blue Dot photo, with Earth seen as a tiny blue spot amidst a vast backdrop of space and bands of light—reminds us that all of humanity's thoughts, passions, and achievements are contained in that tiny blue speck. When we look from that perspective, it's not difficult to recognize that we are part of a collective body. The Pale Blue Dot photo offers an opportunity for us to shift perspectives and free ourselves from our normal way of looking.

Thầy's teaching on the individual and the collective helps us recognize that identity—our identification as an "individual"—is just a convention. Our present-moment experience has always been submerged in a flow of collective consciousness. We have always been part of that stream, even before we were born, and we will always be a part of it. As we have seen, what we call "death" is just a continuation; that collective flow of conscious experience goes on.

Likewise, all of our thoughts are always contributing to a collective understanding. We are affected by collective consciousness, and we also influence it—the boundary between individual and collective is a fiction. With mindfulness, we can see how our actions shape the nature of that collective stream. We begin to notice the obstacles—hatred, greed, and delusion—that disturb the flow from moving in a wholesome direction. That's why it's so apt that the Buddha used the metaphor of "entering the stream" for someone who has unshakeable confidence in the practice. We are actually already in the stream—we just didn't realize it. We were still holding on to the limiting concept of ourselves as individuals, like somebody snagged on a branch in the flow of a river.

P. L.

Manifestation

As we have seen, only when the seeds hidden in the depths of our store consciousness mature and manifest in our mind do we become aware of them. When our anger and sorrow are dormant, we cannot see them. But when we become angry, our face reddens, our voice rises; the seed of anger has ripened, and we notice it. The seeds of anger were there before we became angry, but they were hidden in our store consciousness. If we had said, "I am not angry," this wouldn't have been correct. The seeds of anger were there even though they had not yet manifested.

All manifestations of phenomena arise from our store consciousness. Store consciousness manifests itself into mental formations and physical formations—our sense organs of eyes, ears, nose, tongue, and body and their objects of forms, sounds, smells, tastes, and tactile sensations.[12]

---

12 As there is a continuum from individual to collective consciousness, there is no separation between seeds in the individual and the collective.

Like all of the seeds in our store consciousness, all manifestations bear the marks of the
individual and the collective. All physical manifestations, such as trees, grass, mountains, rivers,
and our own bodies; and all psychological manifestations, such as anger, sadness, fear, and anxiety—are manifestations with both individual and
collective aspects. There is no manifestation of
a phenomenon that is purely individual or purely
collective.

When we light a candle, many places are illu-
minated—the immediate area around the candle,
then the area a little further away, then even further away. When we light a second candle, it also
projects the same three areas of light. And in each
of these spheres of light, the light of the other
candle enters with varying intensity. Once we've
lit the second candle, there is not a single area
of light that comes from only one candle. There
is always the light of the other candle in it. The
different spheres of light do not have only an individual manifestation; they also have a collective
manifestation.

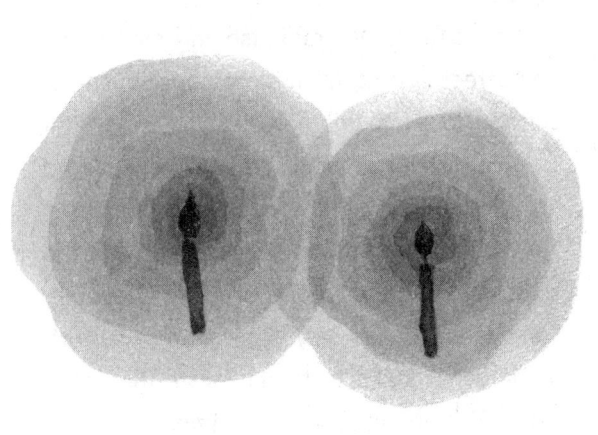

Consciousness of Something

PHÁP LƯU

In the previous section, Thầy says that all manifestations of phenomena—including trees, grass, mountains, and rivers—arise from store consciousness. On first blush, this may sound odd—trees arising from store consciousness. But let's look into this.

For millions of years, humans have played an integral role in how our world manifests. Take fruit. Paleoanthropology tells us that the sweetest fig in the jungles of Africa a few million years ago was only as sweet as a carrot.[13] It's largely thanks to human taste that cultivated fruit got sweeter; very simply, since we favored the trees with sweeter fruit, we prop-

---

13 See Lieberman, D. E. (2013) *The story of the human body : evolution, health, and disease.* First edition. New York: Pantheon Books.

14 For one of many examples of this, see the genetic research on selecting watermelon for sweetness here: Guo, S., Zhao, S., Sun, H. et al. "Resequencing of 414 cultivated and wild watermelon accessions identifies selection for fruit quality traits." *Nature Genetics* 51, 1616–1623 (2019). https://doi.org/10.1038/

agated them.[14] In this way, the fruit co-evolved with the taste in the consciousness of human beings who were eating the fruit. This is a straightforward way in which manifestations of the "natural world"—trees, grass, and so on—co-arise with human consciousness. The same can be said for animals that developed in close proximity to humans, such as domesticated dogs and cats.

Going deeper, we see that mind and object of mind—including things we normally think of as "outside" ourselves—co-arise simultaneously. Consciousness is always consciousness of something. We cannot talk about consciousness without an object of consciousness.

As soon as there's perception of an object, the subject experiencing that perception is also there. Subject and object co-arise together. Vijñāna is a Sanskrit word that can be translated as "consciousness" or "mind." The "vi" part of this word can mean "to separate" or "to cut."

Consciousness is the manifestation of subject and object and thereby cuts the experience in two—into the object experienced and the subject experiencing it. The tree, for example, only arises as a separate phenomenon called "tree" when we have a conscious experience of it as such. The subject and object of that experience are both impermanent; they co-arise and dissolve together. This is an aspect of what Thầy means in chapter two by the "cinematographic nature of consciousness": in any moment, subject and object arise, there's an incident of consciousness, and then they dissolve. It all happens—the arising and passing away of subject and object of consciousness—in rapid succession.

P. L.

Our Actions Need Time to Mature

Maturation is another way of describing store consciousness. You put all the seeds into one container—store consciousness—and wait until every perception, feeling, and mental formation is manifested through maturation.

The Sanskrit word for maturation, *vipāka*, can be translated as "ripening." A seed always needs the right amount of time and the right conditions in order to ripen and bear fruit. When it matures, a seed transforms into a form of being that is the true manifestation of its qualities: for example, an orange blossom produces an orange. The blossom needs the proper time and conditions in order to become an orange that we can eat. Similarly, an act needs time in order to ripen. Our actions, our karma—what we say, think, and do—need time to mature. When they manifest, they manifest in participation with other consciousnesses.[15]

---

15 Eye, ear, nose consciousness and so on.

The ripening of phenomena happens in three ways:

1. **Ripening at different times.** Suppose we pick a custard apple, a bunch of bananas, and a jackfruit and put them away. The custard apple will ripen first, then the bananas, and finally the jackfruit. The seeds that our parents, grandparents, and friends sow and water in us always ripen sooner or later. There is no need to ask, "Why am I not transformed when I have studied the Buddha's teachings for so long? Why do I still not feel peace and joy when I have practiced walking meditation for so many years?" Each seed ripens in its own time. Our practice is simply to water the positive seeds in ourselves. We should have confidence that if we continue to water a certain seed, it will germinate and grow.[16]

---

16 In the next chapter we learn concrete ways—Right Diligence and appropriate attention—to put these teachings into practice for our transformation and healing.

2. **Ripening of different varieties.** An unripe banana becomes a ripe banana—it can never become a ripe custard apple.

3. **Ripening and changing.** When something ripens, many of its aspects change completely. An unripe orange is green and sour. A ripe one is orange and sweet.

Karma Ripening in the Present Moment

To sow a seed is an action-as-cause (*karma-hetu*). When the action-as-cause ripens, it becomes an action-as-result, or action-fruit (*karma-phala*). Maturation means the conclusion of all the actions-as-cause upon their ripening. When we look deeply, we see that our own psychology and physiology, our happiness and our suffering, are all actions-as-result in the present moment of actions-as-cause from the past. Looking back, we can see the past actions that were sown as seeds in our store consciousness. Thanks to the wholesome seeds sown by our ancestors, parents, teachers, friends, and our culture, we can now enjoy peace and joy as we practice walking meditation. Looking in the present, we see that if we continue to water and sow these wholesome seeds, our peace and joy will be greater in the future.

When we look deeply at our body and mind, we see the level of happiness, ease, and freedom in ourselves. Then we slowly shed light on what we have done in the past, the people who have helped us, the things we have put into practice that today bring us this sense of happiness, ease, and freedom. And we also look into what actions-as-cause we have made that result in our being angry, sad, and jealous. To find the seeds from actions done in the past, we need only to look at the fruits in the present moment.

Emancipation—participation in the realm of joy and peace—is a matter of touching and transforming the seeds, of helping the positive seeds grow. We don't need to die in order to be reborn and have a new being. A few weeks or months of mindfulness practice can help ripen the whole-some seeds in us and bring about a new life here and now. By taking care of our seeds—planting and watering the good ones, not helping negative ones to manifest—we are on the path of matura-tion. I have seen people who, after only three or four days of practice, transformed so much they seemed to be entirely new beings. They could go home and reconcile with members of their family and restore the happiness they deserve. The seeds of transformation and healing in them were well taken care of, and maturation could take place quickly. We too are capable of producing a new being from the seeds in our consciousness, of living in a happier and more positive way. There is no reason to think we cannot.

5

Do We Know How to Live?

MOST OF US WASTE OUR LIFE. We don't know how to live. We must learn today how to receive beautifully and create a beautiful continuation; how to live deeply so that we can have happiness, peace, and freedom in every moment of our life.

Today is very precious; we do not know for sure if we will have tomorrow or not. We must evaluate the quality of our life and take control of it. We are the authors; we are our own masters.

Reestablishing Sovereignty: The Five Universal Mental Formations

PHÁP LƯU

In chapter four, Thầy explored in-depth the mental processes by which seeds manifest in mind consciousness and become our continuation as action. It's important to recognize that we can influence this process. With mindfulness, we ensure that our best qualities continue into the future. In this way we re-establish sovereignty over our body and mind, starting now.

The Five Universal Mental Formations—contact, perception, feeling, attention, and volition—are where we can intervene in every instant at the level of the mind. They are called universal because they are mental formations present in any moment of consciousness. Since every Universal Mental Formation is required for conscious experience, if you remove any one of them, you remove a necessary condition for that experience to take place.

Intervening at the level of the Five Universals means we no longer need to push away or suppress unwholesome thoughts. We just remove a condition for that kind of thinking to arise. For instance, if we turn away from the image of an attractive body, one that could water the seed of sexual desire in us, we remove the contact with that image. Eyes and object no longer come in contact to bring about conscious experience of that alluring body. This is how we establish the "guardian at the six gates" that Thầy discussed in chapter one.

Perception, another of these Five Universals, means having a concept, an idea, about the object of sense contact. It may include giving that object a name: flower, snake, and so on. But often our perceptions are incorrect. What we think is a snake may only be a rope. We all have hidden biases and our perceptions about another person, for instance, may be stimulated by things like the color of their skin, the situation in which we meet them, their size, or their tone of voice. Perhaps a traumatic experience from the past gets triggered and colors our perception. When we're mindful, we're able to see that perception is just perception—we don't get lost in an entire story about what we're perceiving, and we interrupt a whole line of thinking that may otherwise have produced a disastrous causal chain plunging us into an abyss of despair.

Feelings—pleasant, unpleasant, or neutral—are often a product of our perception, and this interaction can become a habit; certain perceptions tend to give rise to certain feelings, over and over again. By shining the light of mindfulness on these feelings—on our pain, pleasure, aversion, and so on—we can take care of and transform them. Looking deeply into the difficult feeling, we can see the perceptions that gave rise to it and stop them.

Attention is another crucial point of intervention. If an unwholesome thought arises in the mind, we can remove our attention from it and allow the thought to dissipate. We can choose to focus on something wholesome instead—the gentle rise and fall of our breathing or our body's solid presence on the cushion. Doing so, we remove a necessary condition for that unwholesome thought to continue—our attention. We aren't aggressive, we don't push the thought away, we simply turn our attention elsewhere. This practice is called appropriate attention.

Lastly, there is volition. We know that our volition can have a powerful impact; it can influence others and the world well beyond our immediate sphere of concern. Our daily action feeds our volition, and our volition feeds our actions. We might have the intention to act in certain ways, but our daily behavior can subvert that intention. We may have dreams about living a more wholesome way of life, but if we don't act on them, we might find ourselves helpless when a difficult situation arises.

When we go on a mindfulness retreat, we're strengthening our volition to take care of ourselves and others. As that volition becomes stronger, when a challenge arises, we know what to do: come back to our body and practice what we learned on the retreat.

But if we don't train our volition, we may react in anger and blame and find ourselves judging others in situations of adversity. Our volition requires nourishment, and we nourish it with our practice.

It's very important to observe directly these processes going on, how these aspects of our experience—contact, perception, feeling, attention, and volition—play out and not just know them in theory. By doing so, we touch a deeper level of our experience in the present moment. In what follows, Thay offers two ways of working with the Five Universal Mental Formations: Right Diligence and appropriate attention.

P. L.

The Four Steps of Right Diligence

The practices of mindful walking, breathing, and smiling bring well-being, peace, and happiness. We don't need to practice intensively, with a lot of effort, just regularly and diligently. The term *samyak pradhāna* is sometimes translated as Right Effort. I prefer the word "diligence" to "effort" because effort can make you tired. Many people who practice very intensively for a few weeks become tired and subsequently abandon the practice altogether. The practice should be enjoyable; we should practice diligently but with ease.

Right Diligence, an important aspect of the Noble Eightfold Path, means to practice mindfulness in such a way that we water the positive seeds within us and allow the negative seeds to rest. The Buddha described Right Diligence in four steps, and these four steps inter-are; each step contains the other three.

Buddhist psychology considers consciousness to have two main parts: mind and store. The lower level of our consciousness, called store consciousness, contains all the seeds: seeds of well-being like love, compassion, and joy and seeds of ill-being, like anger, fear, and despair. When a seed is watered it comes up to the upper level called mind consciousness. Mind consciousness is like the living room, and store consciousness is like the basement. Once in mind consciousness, we no longer call it a seed but a mental formation.

The first step in Right Diligence is to try our best not to allow the unbeneficial seeds to manifest. We must be skillful and attentive in allowing these seeds to sleep quietly in our store consciousness. We don't go down and set them off because when we wake them up, they may cause trouble.

If a seed of ill-being has already manifested as a mental formation, we can help it go back down to sleep again as a seed in store consciousness. This is the second aspect of Right Diligence. When a seed manifests in mind consciousness and stays there for a long time, the seed grows stronger at the base. So if an unbeneficial mental formation manifests, don't allow it to stay too long. One way is to invite a beneficial seed to come up and replace it.

To illustrate this practice, the Buddha uses the image of a carpenter's peg. To join two pieces of wood, the carpenter makes a hole in each, aligns the holes, and drives in a peg. But if a peg becomes rotten, he changes the peg by using a new peg to drive the old one out. Similarly, if we don't want to keep watching a particular film or television program, we replace it with another one; we change the channel.

If we don't like anger or despair, why sit there and suffer? When an unbeneficial mental formation manifests, the practitioner should know how to replace it with a good one. There are positive seeds in us of compassion, love, joy, and peace—invite them up. Doing this can change the situation right away. It's a pleasant practice; you don't have to fight or suppress the other mental formation to do this.

The third aspect of Right Diligence is to invite beneficial seeds to come up from store consciousness. Think of a beneficial seed as you would a friend you haven't seen for a while. You know that their presence in your living room would bring a lot of joy, so why not send them an invitation? That friend—the capacity to be happy, joyful, and compassionate—is in you and always available. Joy and happiness are always possible. We should invite them into our living room often. By giving the beneficial things a chance to manifest, we can create a feeling of joy, happiness, serenity, peace, or forgiveness. The fourth aspect of Right Diligence is, when something beneficial arises, to keep it there as long as possible. When a good friend has come to your living room, you want them to stay. The longer a beneficial seed stays in the living room, the stronger it will become. When good things arise, try to keep them in mind consciousness. At the base, that good seed will continue to grow, and next time it will manifest more easily. Sometimes you don't even have to invite that seed up—it comes up naturally into your mind consciousness. Through the practice of Right Diligence, happiness becomes a habit. If the seeds of happiness and love become strong, they will manifest regularly by themselves, without invitation, and we will welcome them.

These four aspects of Right Diligence take practice. Keep the difficult seeds sleeping down there; don't invite them up. But if they have manifested, try your best to let them return to store consciousness as soon as possible. Invite up the good things that haven't manifested. And when they manifest, invite them to stay longer. That is the true meaning of diligence. It can bring so much happiness.

The Habit of Mindfulness

Our happiness depends on the good habits we develop. Some habit energies have taken thousands of years to form, but what we inherit does not only come from what others have done in the past. It matters what we do in the present. Every word we speak and every act we perform will determine how we are.

When we are mindful, when we are aware

of all our actions of body, speech, and mind, we can choose to act, speak, and think in wholesome ways rather than in harmful ways. Mindfulness is the best habit that we can develop. With the energy of mindfulness, we can avoid watering seeds of anger, craving, and delusion in our store consciousness and we can water seeds of joy, peace, and wisdom.

In Buddhism we are urged to practice appropriate attention, *yoniśo manaskāra*. For example, when you hear someone inviting a bell, you bring your attention to the sound of the bell and you say, "I listen, I listen; this wonderful sound brings me back to my true home." And because your attention is turned toward a wholesome object, you water the beautiful seeds in you. You establish yourself in the here and now, you touch the depth of your being, and you receive healing and peace—that is appropriate attention. You can arrange your house, your living room, your schedule in such a way that you have many opportunities for your mind to touch what is wholesome and positive. Many people download a bell of mindfulness onto their phone or computer, for instance, so that every ten or fifteen minutes they hear a sound of the bell. With the sound of the bell, they stop what they are doing, come back to their breath, and enjoy smiling, following their breathing, and not getting lost in their work. That is the practice of yoniso manaskara, appropriate attention.

Enjoyment can become a habit. Some of us only have the habit of suffering. Others among us have cultivated the habit of smiling and being happy, and this is the best thing we can cultivate. So please enjoy walking mindfully, enjoy sitting in mindfulness. We enjoy sitting and walking for ourselves, for our ancestors, for our parents, our friends, our beloved ones, and for our so-called enemies. Walking like a buddha—that is our practice. We don't need to learn and understand all the sutras, all the Buddha's written teachings, in order to be able to walk like a buddha. We don't need anything more than our two feet and our awareness. We can drink our tea mindfully, brush our teeth mindfully; we can breathe in mindfully, make a step mindfully. And it can be done with a lot of joy and without any fighting or any effort. It's a matter of enjoyment.

Habit energies are our only true belongings, the only heritage we will continue to own when we die. Everything else—our loved ones, our home, our college degrees—we must leave behind. All we take with us is our habit energies, and we can't choose which ones to take; we have to take them all.

How We Continue Is Up to Us

PHÁP LƯU

Right Diligence and appropriate attention are both concrete ways of working with the Five Universals mentioned above. Take volition, for example. The volition to bring mindfulness into our daily lives has a direct effect on our attention. With that volition, we choose to place our attention on objects that nourish our seeds of peace, joy, and gratitude. This is to choose the path of appropriate attention. And nourishing wholesome mental formations with appropriate attention, choosing to place our attention here and not there, is also the practice of Right Diligence. Shining the light of mindfulness on our feeling of happiness, we appreciate that happiness has manifested in our conscious awareness, and we make room for it to stay for a while.

With Right Diligence and appropriate attention, we can generate wholesome habits.

If we train ourselves to place our attention on our in-breath and out-breath, mindfulness of breathing becomes a habit. And with the habit of mindful breathing, when anger begins to manifest, we recognize it right away. We shine the light of mindfulness on the seed of anger as it manifests in our mind consciousness, we take care of it and let it go back down into its seed form in store consciousness. We can get very precise with this technique as we deepen our mindfulness practice—it's like having a microscope with a finely ground lens at our disposal. We can see what anger looks like in its seed form, when it's just starting to sprout, rather than after it becomes overwhelming, so we can more easily take care of it.

Imagine an acorn that becomes an oak tree. When an acorn sprouts in the spring, a little root pokes out. And with a slight nudge of our foot, we can abort that acorn's process of rooting in the soil. But of course, once it has taken root, once it has established itself in the ground and become a sapling, it's much more difficult to uproot. How much more so when it becomes a massive tree after many decades of growth! That's the difference between anger in its seed form and anger after it takes over our mind. If we allow the seed of anger to manifest over and over again in our daily interactions, it becomes deeply rooted in our consciousness. At that point, like the big oak tree, that anger is very difficult to remove.

In fact, anger itself—and all emotions—arise and pass away rather quickly if they aren't reinforced. For our emotions to endure, they need to be nourished—fed by our perceptions. The cogitating aspect of the mind—the part that just keeps thinking—continues to drip-feed our emotions. And as we steadily feed our anger, we may develop an underlying resentment that taints our experience of daily life. With the practice of Right Diligence, we can shine the light of awareness directly on the sprouting seed of anger and invite it to go back down.

We train ourselves not to allow anger to take over our mind. We practice letting go when perceptions arise that feed the seed of anger in our consciousness. This is the practice of Right Diligence. We learn how to invite back down any unwholesome mental formations that arise in mind consciousness. When they manifest, we don't continue to feed them with our perceptions, even if we consider those perceptions to be true.

A good question to ask ourselves regarding our perceptions is, "Are you sure?" If we can generate some humility, we can see that many of our perceptions are quite limited. We see things from just one angle, and we take that one angle to be the whole truth. For instance, someone may be trying to help us, they may be well-intentioned, but their words touch the seed of anger in us for one reason or another. They may use unskillful language, for instance, and because of that, we are unable to receive whatever good may be in what they say. If we're able to take care of our perceptions—if we see our perception for what it is and not put too much stock in its accuracy—we can stop the cycle right away, cutting off the source of nutriment feeding the underlying resentment.

How we continue in the world through our thoughts, speech, and actions is up to us. There is so much we can do to influence how we show up in the world—practicing Right Diligence and appropriate attention are two examples. It takes time to become skillful at working with our own mind, but it's the best thing we can do for ourselves and each other, now and for generations to come.

If we can keep our mind wide and open, we can orient ourselves in the direction of transformation and healing. We can produce the kinds of actions of body, speech, and mind that are beneficial for ourselves and others. These are our continuation, our rebirth. In each moment, we begin anew. We are born again, over and over—every time we choose not to act out of blame or judgement and instead act from understanding and compassion.

Non-fear is crucial for us to practice in this way. We need real determination to stop feeding our anger, to stop feeding our jealousy and despair, especially when our habit energy pushes us in the direction of ignorance. If we don't make the choice to go in a wholesome direction, we risk forgetting completely others' humanity. And that forgetting can lead to out-right destruction—war, genocide, and other horrible things that turn our global situation into a living hell. Practicing in each moment to ensure a beautiful continuation is an urgent kind of peace work; the future of our species and our planet depends on it.

P. L.

Insight in Our Daily Life

One day while walking in the park, I asked a leaf whether it was afraid to fall since it was autumn and the other leaves were falling. The leaf told me, "During the whole spring and summer I was very alive. I worked hard and helped nourish the tree, and much of me is in the tree. Please do not think that I am just this form, because this leaf form is only a tiny part of me. I am the whole tree. I know that I am already inside the tree, and when I go back to the soil, I will continue to nourish the tree. That is why I do not worry. As I drop from the branch and float down to the ground, I will wave to the tree and tell her, 'I will see you again very soon.'"

Suddenly I had a kind of insight. You have to *see* life. You shouldn't say life *of* the leaf but life *in* the leaf and life *in* the tree. My life is just life, and you can see it in me and in the tree. I saw the leaf leave the branch and float down to the soil, dancing joyfully, because as it floated it saw itself already there in the tree. It was so happy. I bowed my head, and I knew that we have a lot to learn from the leaf because it was not afraid; it knew that nothing can be born and nothing can die.

It would be wrong to think that what falls to the ground and dies is the whole of the leaf. During the nine months that it lived, the leaf travelled far. It has breathed and produced oxygen, which has entered into us human beings. When we practice walking meditation, we receive nourishment from the leaves as we breathe the fresh air, which in part is made by the leaves. The leaf, which has now fallen to the ground, has entered both us and the tree it fell from. It is not easy to see all the places the leaf has gone. We should not identify the leaf cadaver we see on the ground as being the whole of the leaf. Only with this insight can we truly see the leaf, which is present everywhere.

After many months of superb work nourishing the tree, nourishing other species, providing shade, and making life beautiful, the leaf lets go and gracefully falls to the ground, without any fear, because it knows it has gone out in many directions. It does not identify itself with the form that is floating down to earth, because what is floating down is just a small part of itself that will become one with the earth; in the future it may become a leaf or a flower again. There is nothing to attain and nothing is lost.

When we look into a leaf we should look deeply like this in order to see that the leaf is not just present in the leaf. It is also present in the tree and in all other phenomena. Once we are able to see in this way, our grief and our sorrow will disappear.

Offering the Gift of Non-fear

If we have a real experience of Right View, not just a theoretical understanding of it, we can help many people. The realization that our body is not a separate self is very important. Our body is continued outside the body, and once we have seen the true nature of this physical body, its birth and eventual death, its coming and going can no longer touch us. With the insight of no birth and no death, we can help others be at peace.

Anathapindika was a lay disciple who had always given a lot of support to the Buddha and the community of monks. When he was about to pass away and was in great pain, he was given teachings by the Venerable Śāriputra to help him let go of ideas of self and life span. After Śāriputra guided Anathapindika in a meditation on the Buddha, the Dharma, and the Sangha to nourish the seeds of joy in him, he began to offer the cream of the Buddha's teachings: "Friend Anathapindika, please meditate like this: These eyes are not me. I am not caught in these eyes." He went from eyes to ears, nose, tongue, body and mind; to form, sound, smell, taste, touch and objects of mind; then from eye consciousness to mind consciousness. "All these things are not me. I have no need to be caught by them."

Śāriputra continued, "Friend Anathapindika, all things exist because of causes and conditions. When the causes and conditions for them cease to exist, they no longer exist. The true nature of things is not to be born and not to die, not to come and not to go." When Anathapindika heard these teachings, he understood them immediately. He knew he had only a short time left to live, and that was enough motivation for him to put the teachings into practice without delay. When he practiced in this way, tears of happiness started to run down his cheeks, and Anathapindika passed away in peace.

We, too, are fortunate to have the cream of the teachings available to us. We have to practice letting go of our ideas in order to see life everywhere, beyond space and time. We should not wait until our last moments to begin to contemplate that this body is not myself. Please look deeply into this truth.

Seeing that we are the sun, we give up the candle's habit of fearing the wind. Seeing that life has no boundaries, we give up all imprisoning divisions. We see ourselves and our lives everywhere. Let go in order to be everything and to be completely free.

Sources

EPIGRAPHS

Material for the epigraphs comes from talks given by Thích Nhất Hạnh on July 12, 2008 and June 17, 2014 and from *Old Path, White Clouds* (Parallax Press, 1987).

CHAPTER ONE

Material for Chapter One comes from talks given by Thích Nhất Hạnh on July 22, 2002; March 24, 2004; and August 5, 2005. Additional material for this chapter comes from *Buddha Mind, Buddha Body: Walking Toward Enlightenment* (Parallax Press, 2003) and *Good Citizens: Creating Enlightened Society* (Parallax Press, 2008).

CHAPTER TWO

Material for Chapter Two comes from talks given by Thích Nhất Hạnh on July 22, 2002; March 24, 2004; June 21, 2009; October 8, 2013; October 16, 2013; November 22, 2012; June 3, 2014; June 20, 2014; and June 21, 2014.

CHAPTER THREE

Material for Chapter Three comes from talks given by Thích Nhất Hạnh on March 24, 2004; December 31, 2009; January 7, 2011; June 3, 2014; June 5, 2014; and June 20, 2014. Additional material for this chapter comes from *Transformation and Healing: Sutra on the*

Four Establishments of Mindfulness (Parallax Press, 2002), and *The Other Shore: A New Translation of the Heart Sutra with Commentaries* (Palm Leaves Press, 2017).

CHAPTER FOUR

All material for Chapter Four comes from *Understanding Our Mind* (Parallax Press, 2002).

CHAPTER FIVE

Material for Chapter Five comes from talks given by Thích Nhất Hạnh on March 24, 2004; February 6, 2014; and June 14, 2014. Additional material for this chapter comes from *Understanding Our Mind* (Parallax Press, 2002), *Buddha Mind, Buddha Body: Walking Toward Enlightenment* (Parallax Press, 2003), *Good Citizens: Creating Enlightened Society* (Parallax Press, 2008), *Breathe, You Are Alive!: Sutra on the Full Awareness of Breathing* (Parallax Press, 2008), and *The Other Shore: A New Translation of the Heart Sutra with Commentaries* (Palm Leaves Press, 2017).

THE ZEN DOORS SERIES

The Zen Doors series distills and explains some of Buddhism's most popular, yet often misunderstood, concepts. Fresh commentaries from the next generation of Zen teachers trained by Thích Nhất Hạnh bring his groundbreaking teachings into everyday life. The series honors Thích Nhất Hạnh's lifetime commitment to awakening for all—across cultural, educational, and experiential divides.

About THÍCH NHẤT HẠNH

World-renowned spiritual teacher and peace activist Thích Nhất Hạnh was born in Vietnam in 1926 and became a Zen Buddhist monk at the age of sixteen. Over seven decades of teaching, he published more than one hundred books, which have sold millions of copies. Exiled from Vietnam in 1966 for promoting peace, his teachings on Buddhism as a path to social and political transformation are responsible for introducing mindfulness to Western society and culture.

About BROTHER PHÁP LƯU

Brother Pháp Lưu (Brother Stream) ordained as a monk in 2003 and received Transmission of the Lamp from Zen Master Thích Nhất Hạnh to teach in 2011. He serves on the Advisory Board of the Thích Nhất Hạnh Center for Mindfulness in Public Health at the Harvard T. H. Chan School of Public Health. He has edited several of Thích Nhất Hạnh's books and coauthored a book with Brother Pháp Xả called *Hiking Zen.*

Monastics and visitors practice the art of mindful living in the tradition of Thich Nhat Hanh at our mindfulness practice centers around the world. To reach any of these communities, or for information about how individuals, couples, and families can join in a retreat, please contact:

Plum Village
33580 Dieulivol, France
plumvillage.org

Blue Cliff Monastery
Pine Bush, NY 12566, USA
bluecliffmonastery.org

**European Institute of
Applied Buddhism**
D-51545 Waldbröl, Germany
eiab.eu

Healing Spring Monastery
77510 Verdelot,
France
healingspringmonastery.org

**Asian Institute of
Applied Buddhism**
Ngong Ping, Lantau Island
Hong Kong
pvfhk.org

Mountain Spring Monastery
Bilpin, Victoria 2758
Australia
mountainspringmonastery.org

Magnolia Grove Monastery
Batesville, MS 38606, USA
magnoliagrovemonastery.org

Deer Park Monastery
Escondido, CA 92026, USA
deerparkmonastery.org

Thailand Plum Village
Nakhon Ratchasima
30130 Thailand
thaiplumvillage.org

Maison de l'Inspir
77510 Villeneuve-sur-Bellot
France
maisondelinspir.org

**Nhap Luu-Stream
Entering Monastery**
Porcupine Ridge, Victoria 3461
Australia
nhapluu.org

The Mindfulness Bell, a journal of the art of mindful living in the tradition of Thich Nhat Hanh, is published two times a year by our community. To subscribe or to see the worldwide directory of sanghas (local mindfulness groups), visit mindfulnessbell.org.

Further Resources

For information about our international community
plumvillage.org

To find an online sangha
plumline.org

Talks and practices on the Plum Village app
plumvillage.app

THICH NHAT HANH FOUNDATION

planting seeds of Compassion

The Thich Nhat Hanh Foundation works to continue the mindful teachings and practice of Zen Master Thich Nhat Hanh, in order to foster peace and transform suffering in all people, animals, plants, and our planet. Through donations to the Foundation, thousands of generous supporters ensure the continuation of Plum Village practice centers and monastics around the world, bring transformative practices to those who otherwise would not be able to access them, support local mindfulness initiatives, and bring humanitarian relief to communities in crisis in Vietnam.

By becoming a supporter, you join many others who want to learn and share these life-changing practices of mindfulness, loving speech, deep listening, and compassion for oneself, each other, and the planet.

For more information on how you can help support mindfulness around the world, or to subscribe to the Foundation's monthly newsletter with teachings, news, and global retreats, visit tnhf.org.

Parallax Press

Parallax Press, a nonprofit publisher founded by Zen
Master Thich Nhat Hanh, publishes books and media
on the art of mindful living and Engaged Buddhism. We
are committed to offering teachings that help transform
suffering and injustice. Our aspiration is to contribute
to collective insight and awakening, bringing about
a more joyful, healthy, and compassionate society.

View our entire library at parallax.org.